IN THIS VERY HOUR

Devotions for Your Time of Need

IN THIS VERY HOUR

LOSS OF A JOB

Devotions for Your Time of Need

MARTY SCHOENLEBER

BROADMAN & HOLMAN PUBLISHERS

Nashville, Tennessee

© 1994
by Broadman & Holman Publishers
All rights reserved

Printed in the United States of America

4253-76
0-8054-5376-8

Dewey Decimal Classification: 242.4
Subject Heading:
DEVOTIONAL LITERATURE // UNEMPLOYED
Library of Congress Card Catalog Number: 94-15652

Unless otherwise noted, Scripture quotations are from the Holy Bible, *New International Version,* copyright © 1973, 1978, 1984 by International Bible Society. Scripture quotations marked NASB are from the *New American Standard Bible,* © 1960, 1962, 1963, 1968, 1971, 1972, 1973, 1975, 1977, by the Lockman Foundation.

Library of Congress Cataloging-in-Publication Data
Schoenleber, Marty, 1955–
  Devotions for your time of need.
Loss of a job / by Marty Schoenleber, Jr.
      p. cm. — (In this very hour)
  Includes bibliographical references.
  ISBN 0-8054-5376-8
  1. Unemployed—Prayer-books and devotions—English. 2. Church work with the unemployed.   I. Title. II. Series.
BV4596.U53S36 1994
242'.4—dc20   94-15652
                                                          CIP

*To my bride of ten years
who believed in me
and knew this day would come*

Contents

Prologue:	Recognizing the Process	1
1.	Establish a Basis for Hope	7
2.	Develop Wise Ears	8
3.	Remain Human in the Search	9
4.	Don't Look Back	10
5.	Maintain Your Integrity I	11
6.	Avoid the Slug I	12
7.	Treasure the Truth I	13
8.	Treasure the Truth II	14
9.	Keep Your Hope in Front	15
10.	Know When to Be Silent	16
11.	Practice the Art of Remaining	17
12.	Avoid Things that Destroy Hope	18
13.	Avoid the Slug II	19
14.	Labor for the Profit	20
15.	Pave the Way to the Next Job	21
16.	Find the Right Plan	22
17.	Find a Biblical Friend	23

18.	Keep Your Head and Your Heart	24
19.	Maintain Your Integrity II	25
20.	The Sluggard Returns!	26
21.	Trusting a Powerful God	27
22.	Avoid Debt	28
23.	Avoid Bad Company	29
24.	Out of Bed and into the Shower!	30
25.	Over-Promotion Pitfalls I	31
26.	Over-Promotion Pitfalls II	32
27.	Work Your Network	33
28.	Be Patient	33
29.	Control Your Emotions	34
30.	Lessons in Building a Better Future	35
31.	There Are Others Like You	36
Epilogue:	Surviving the Chaos of the Hunt	38
Resources:	Suggested Reading	43

PROLOGUE

Recognizing the Process

I take solace from the fact that my experience is not unlike that of many others in America. I had a job I liked, a job in which I had experienced a measure of success.

But someone else came along who could work for less, who was better trained, who was more experienced, who had more education. Before long, the writing was on the wall—there would be no place for me in the future of the company.

It happens to millions of Americans, male and female, young and not so young. It happens to school teachers like me and factory workers and engineers and secretaries and major league baseball players and NFL football players.

If you are reading this book, the odds are that it has happened to you recently. You could have been Betty or Bob or Carol whom you will meet in the pages that follow. I'll tell you how I met Betty.

Betty's Story

"Marty, I need your help," a church member said to me in a frantic telephone call. "My next door neighbor, Betty, has been at my house for the last two hours and I don't know how to help her. The bank just told Betty that her house would be repossessed on Friday of next week. She is divorced and has no family in the area. She has been unemployed for two years. In addition to all of that, Betty is a diabetic with a sickly fifteen-year-old daughter. What should I do? What do I tell her?"

When this call came I was working on my next sermon. Almost instantly, three things became very clear. One, the sermon could wait. Two, whatever I said next would be perceived as *the* thing to do. Third, I didn't have a clue about what to tell the anxious person on the other end of the line.

For months I had been preaching and teaching that our new church plant was not interested in "playing church." I boldly told our members that we were going to be a church that got involved in the "dirtier, messier, less glamorous ministries" of working with the poor, the unemployed, the lonely, and the forgotten. I said that we were going to be multi-racial, multi-cultural, multi-socio/economic in our intent and in the development of every ministry of the church—big words that were being tested in the crucible of reality.

Despite my own near panic at not knowing what to say, it was an exciting call. It meant that someone in the congregation was catching the vision. It also meant that my own commitment and vision were going to be challenged and expanded.

In October of 1991, I and a band of pioneering (some would say, crazy) hearts planted a church in a blue-collar Illinois community with rising unemployment. On the first Sunday, 147 people showed up to see what it was all about. We were ecstatic, but it soon became apparent that we had stepped onto a sinking ship.

Almost two thirds of the people at that service were "unchurched." One woman told me that she had not been to a church for twenty-seven years. A man told me he had never been to church; another told me that this was his first church appearance in fifteen years. As the first few weeks passed, my counseling load grew. Eight couples had come to our first service because their marriages were in various stages of disintegration. New Song Church was their last hope.

There were others looking for hope as well—the unemployed, the underemployed, the nearly homeless, the bankrupt, and the near bankrupt were there. The diversity of the needs were amazing, but two trends soon became clear. One, all of the people we worked with needed hope. Two, all of the people we worked with needed help in their ability to continue to hope.

That's what this book is about, building and sustaining hope in the midst of the loss of one job and the search for a new one. I suspect you will see yourself and your situation in the situations of Betty or Bob or Carol. The epilogue will fill you in on the rest of their stories but each one will sound familiar. Each will tell you that hope and trust in God sustained, guided, and protected him or her. Each will also tell you that trust in God was a good investment.

Carol's Story

Carol was an attractive divorcee in her mid-thirties, struggling to raise eight- and twelve-year-old girls on less than enough income. She was a Christian whose joy in Christ was being beaten down by the tension of too many bills, too little income, too few friends, too many memories, and too meager a hope. Then the bottom fell out.

For five years, Carol scrimped and saved and managed to put herself through nursing school. Juggling the responsibilities of being breadwinner, mother/father, and homemaker was grueling, but now she was steps away from getting the job that had driven and fueled her vision for five years. First, she had to pass her State exam. Study. Pray. Study. Pray. Pray. Study. Pray. Exam. Wait. Pray. Wait. Pray. Passed!

Apply for job. Pray. Wait. Pray. Hired! *What a great place to work,* she thought. *I love my job. Thank You, God, for the opportunity to work here.*

Two months later.

"Carol, you have been a great asset to our office," her supervisor began. "You have performed excellently, and you have brought a spirit of kindness to our office. But we need you to be on call twenty-four hours a day, six days a week."

"But I have children!"

"I know, and I am disappointed too, but that doesn't change the needs we have here. I'm sorry."

"Me too."

Unemployed...

Bob's Story

Bob was an elder at his church, an accomplished musician, the father of three boys, and a competent middle manager at a food processing plant. He was also caught in a numbers game in an age of "downsizing." "Laid off" is the term they used.

An out-placement company was hired to help Bob and others caught in the shuffle find new jobs. Four months of hunting had yielded nothing, however, and it was getting harder and harder to keep up the smile. At times his hope alternated with despair.

"This would be a great company to work for," became "When am I going to get a job?" His ego, stamina, and joy were drained like a flashlight battery. Home was becoming more stressful as well. The two younger boys showed signs of anxiety as the interviews for potential jobs moved further and further away from the comfortable confines of their adolescent years.

The one positive effect was that Bob found his times of prayer richer than he had in years.

"God, help me to present myself well," he prayed often. "Give me wisdom. Enable me to be content in all things. You have enabled me to live in plenty in the past. Enable me to live with less now."

"How's the job hunt going, Bob?" his pastor asked one day.

"Oh, I've got three interviews over the next three weeks, but only one is a callback."

"How's your family taking the process?"

"Pretty well, I guess. We all just wish it would be over."

"The men are praying for you on Tuesday morning, but is there anything else we can be doing?" asked the pastor.

Bob's reply was appreciative but sober. "Not that I know of. Just keep praying, I guess."

"We will, Bob. Hang in there." With a pat on the back, the pastor was gone and Bob was left where he had been for the last four months—jobless. *I need a job soon,* he thought.

1

ESTABLISH A BASIS FOR HOPE

The fear of the LORD is the beginning of knowledge, but fools despise wisdom and discipline.

Proverbs 1:7

No job loss or job search is simple. Living the Christian life, on the other hand, is really very simple. It is simply learning to live our lives for an audience of One, the Sovereign of the Universe. Learning to live for that all-seeing audience is what the fear of the Lord is all about.

REMEMBER: The most important thoughts you have are your thoughts about God. King Solomon knew that, and if you are a Christian you also know it, even if at times you lapse into forgetfulness. Real hope must be centered in the reality of who God is. Reverencing—fearing—God is the beginning of all wisdom. Make up your mind that you are going to live to please God today, no matter what job opportunities come your way.

PRAY: *Lord of hope, I do not want to live a life that despises Your way of wisdom. I don't want to turn my back on anything You want to teach me. Make me a "God-fearer." Make me the kind of person who lives out every thought in Your presence. Give me your perspective in my job search.*

PLAN: Today, I will make it my aim to fear God. I will look for a job with the knowledge that "This is my Father's world." He will guide me. I will trust Him.

2

DEVELOP WISE EARS

My son, if you accept my words and store up my commands within you, turning your ear to wisdom and applying your heart to understanding, and if you call out for insight and cry aloud for understanding and if you look for it as for silver and search for it as for hidden treasure, then you will understand the fear of the LORD and find the knowledge of God.

For the LORD gives wisdom, and from his mouth come knowledge and understanding.

Proverbs 2:1–6

REMEMBER: It is a wise ear that listens to the voice of God. A wise ear is an ear that is tuned to the frequency of His commands. A wise ear is an ear that is eager to apply the "hidden treasure" of the Word of God.

PRAY: *Father, give me wise ears today. Help me to remember Your Word and to organize the whole of my day around its principles. I will trust You today to guide me in my choices, and I will thank You for the path You show.*

PLAN: I'm going to listen only to Christian radio stations in the car as I drive to any job interviews, so I can prepare my heart to be open to God's voice.

3

REMAIN HUMAN IN THE SEARCH

Do not let kindness and truth leave you; Bind them around your neck, write them on the tablet of your heart.

Proverbs 3:3, NASB

You were just rudely treated at an interview. Yesterday the appointment you made and prepared for was canceled—after you drove thirty minutes and canceled another interview. The third receptionist this week greets you with the same yawning, "Please fill this questionnaire out and Mr. Smith will be with you in a minute," that you have heard before. Your bills are piling up. And each employer seems more interested in your resumé than you and your ability to do the job. Kindness gets tested in situations like these.

REMEMBER: A kind heart is an attractive commodity. Obey the Scripture. Write it on your heart; that is, make up your mind that you are going to respond to each situation with kindness. Make sure that the last memory others have of you is the first thing you want them to remember. Be kind with the truth.

PRAY: *Father, it is so hard to be kind when I am treated unfairly. Enable me to make kindness the necklace of my life. Let the people I meet and interview with see a person who displays a generosity of spirit that is attractive in the work force.*

PLAN: I am going to memorize this verse today and make it the content of my thought on my drive to each interview.

4

Don't Look Back

> Let your eyes look straight ahead, fix your gaze directly before you.
>
> *Proverbs 4:25*

Even a bad job can look pretty good when the alternative is no job at all. In hard times the past can become a spellbinding and blinding tyrant, dictating the content of your thoughts and keeping you from seeing the larger picture of what God has for you.

REMEMBER: The New Testament echoes Solomon in its direction to "fix our eyes on Jesus, the author and perfecter of our faith" (Heb. 12:2). Don't look back. You can't get where you are going looking in the rearview mirror. You must fix your gaze on the goal. Keep your hope in front of you. God will not desert you. He will never leave you.

PRAY: *Lord, I need You to guide my vision. Keep me from longing for and moping about the past. My hope is in the supply You will give.*

PLAN: Read the entire fourth chapter of Proverbs. Write down one verse that will help you keep your focus on the character and provision of God. Put the paper in your pocket and carry it with you today.

5

MAINTAIN YOUR INTEGRITY I

For a man's ways are in full view of the Lord, and he examines all his paths.

Proverbs 5:21

An unobstructed view of every way and thought of your heart—that is what God has of you. He is the only One you have to please today. You may think that you have to please a boss, an employer, a parent, a child, a spouse, but the reality is that you need to please an audience of One. Successful job hunting takes the initiative to search for a job under the guidance of the Holy Spirit—and leaves the results to God.

REMEMBER: Everything you do today will be done in the presence of God. Every thought you will think will be scrutinized by the holy eye of God. Remember that He is examining your path today.

PRAY: *Father, You know all my anxious thoughts. Help me to bring each one into submission to Your will.*

PLAN: Today when you struggle with peer pressure or are overly concerned with what others think, learn the principle of living your life simply to please God. Teach others around you by your example to live for an audience of One.

6

Avoid the Slug I

> Go to the ant, you sluggard; consider its ways and be wise! It has no commander, no overseer or ruler, yet it stores its provisions in summer and gathers its food at harvest.
>
> How long will you lie there, you sluggard? When will you get up from your sleep? A little sleep, a little slumber, a little folding of the hands to rest—and poverty will come on you like a bandit and scarcity like an armed man.
>
> *Proverbs 6:7–11*

The mental image of the ant and the sluggard can be a real lesson for our lives. It may be tempting to take time off to "rest," and "take it easy" while you are without a job. But this is the time to begin planning. Even though you are unsure of what the future will bring, you must not lose momentum.

REMEMBER: The slug has no plan; life just happens to him. You can't afford to be slug-like. Like the ant, you need to develop a plan and then you need to work that plan. When you have a plan in place, it becomes a source of great hope and confidence.

PRAY: *Father, I have so much time on my hands that it is difficult sometimes to be disciplined. Use the humor of this passage to keep me from becoming "slug-like." Help me to be disciplined in the pursuit of the job You have for me.*

PLAN: Read—and laugh—at all of the images of the sluggard in the book of Proverbs (see Prov. 13:4; 15:19; 19:24; 20:4; 21:25; 22:13; 24:30; 26:13–16). Then, apply them to your life this week.

7

TREASURE THE TRUTH I

My son, keep my words and store up my commands within you.

Keep my commands and you will live; guard my teachings as the apple of your eye.

Proverbs 7:1–2

"Keeping" words and "storing up commands" sometimes doesn't seem practical in the rush of trying to find a new job. Yet the Word of God cries out, "Keep my commands and you will live."

REMEMBER: Treasure the Word of God. Remember the images in these verses: "keep," "store," "guard," "apple of your eye." Adopt His words as your guide. You will not be disappointed.

PRAY: *Truthful and commanding God, teach me to love Your Word with all my heart. Help me to store and keep and guard Your Word as the apple of my eye. I want to live in light of the truth of Your Word.*

PLAN: Memorize these two verses and ask God to remind you of them throughout the day.

8

TREASURE THE TRUTH II

> Heed instruction and be wise, and do not neglect it.
>
> *Proverbs 8:33, NASB*

I have never read the book, but the title is at least as valuable as the contents. Paul Billheimer's *Don't Waste Your Sorrows* (Christian Literature Crusade, 1977) says a world in just four words. That simple title pierces the veil of my excuses and challenges me when all I want to do is crawl into a corner and cry.

REMEMBER: Don't waste your sorrows. The loss of your job and the tedious and often disappointing search for a new one can be a rich time of learning new things about God, your family, yourself. Make up your mind that you are not going to neglect whatever it is that God wants to teach you through the process of finding a new job.

PRAY: *Lord of wisdom and truth, show me something new today. Lift my heart with the joy of some new discovery about You.*

PLAN: Read the first two chapters of 1 Samuel. Make a list of the attributes/characteristics of God that Hannah refers to in her behavior before God and in her prayer to God.

9

KEEP YOUR HOPE IN FRONT

The fear of the Lord is the beginning of wisdom, and knowledge of the Holy One is understanding.

For through me your days will be many, and years will be added to your life.

Proverbs 9:10–11

There are days when the sense of failure is suffocating. "Why wasn't I considered indispensable?" "What could I have done differently?" "Why couldn't I get along with my boss?" "Why did they let me go?"

REMEMBER: Every journey has to have a beginning. The wisdom journey begins with the fear—reverence, respect, awe—of the Lord. The process that begins with fear ends in life. There is hope in the way and will of God.

PRAY: *Lord of life, help me to keep my perspective in this journey we are traveling together. I want to please You in every thought I have today.*

PLAN: Meditate on the following: How would your life be different if you had a greater reverence and fear of the Lord? Then read Psalm 119:33–40.

10

KNOW WHEN TO BE SILENT

> When words are many, sin is not absent, but he who holds his tongue is wise.
>
> *Proverbs 10:19*

Yesterday's interview went great until you volunteered more information than was required. Somehow you got started on what the work environment was like at your last job and before you knew it, the tone of your comments had deteriorated to complaining. You saw it happen. The interviewer changed position in his seat, and you knew that his perspective toward you had changed as well.

REMEMBER: Your employer needs to know that you are loyal, hardworking, congenial, and qualified to do the job. He doesn't need to know what you feel about the new baseball divisions, the president of the

United States, or health care reform. Converse, be friendly, but stick to the task of earnestly persuading your interviewer that you are the best person for the job. Holding your tongue is a wise thing to do.

PRAY: *Lord, give me discernment in what I say today. Help me to know when to keep my mouth shut. Give me tact and wisdom in all of my responses today.*

PLAN: Read James 3:1–12. Spend at least ten minutes thinking about the illustrations your "older brother" James records there.

11

PRACTICE THE ART OF REMAINING

The truly righteous man attains life, but he who pursues evil goes to his death.

Proverbs 11:19

Sometimes it is easy to doubt that there is any profit in righteousness. It is easy to feel trapped. You know of men and women laid off from their jobs who have already been reemployed. You also know that they lied about the experience and training they had. It seems so unfair. Everyone isn't playing the game by the same rules.

REMEMBER: The righteous man or woman attains life. Appearances can be deceiving. Keep your integrity in front of you. Practice the art of remaining holy before the Lord of glory who calls you to Himself and will yet provide for your needs.

PRAY: *Lord of glory, help me to conquer every thought that threatens my peace. Help me to trust in You.*

PLAN: Read Psalm 73 today. Notice how the perspective of the psalmist changes at verse 17. In your own words, summarize and record on a 3 x 5 card what the writer concluded. Carry it with you today as a reminder of the perspective which conquers doubt, depression, and despair.

12

AVOID THINGS THAT DESTROY HOPE

He who works his land will have abundant food,
but he who chases fantasies lacks judgment.

Proverbs 12:11

It has probably happened to you already. You are in desperate financial straits and suddenly you are inundated with pyramid marketing schemes, lottery advertising, and Uncle Henry's latest get-rich-quick scheme. You know that gambling is just a fantasy, but the temptation to chase that fantasy is clouding your judgment.

REMEMBER: More than once you have been tempted to think you had a better idea than God. You've been wrong before! You may be tempted to think less of

God and His ways during your job search. Resist it. Working at your full-time job of finding a job is your best hope for abundance in life.

PRAY: *Father, give me the stamina to continue this process and to exercise sound judgment in the face of temptation.*

PLAN: Don't buy that lottery ticket you were thinking about!

13

AVOID THE SLUG II

The sluggard craves and gets nothing, but the desires of the diligent are fully satisfied.

Proverbs 13:4

Bobby Knight, Indiana University basketball coach and sometime so-called bad guy, was right about one thing: *It isn't the will to win that makes winners*. No one wakes up in the morning and says they can't wait to ruin their marriage or sabotage their relationship with their kids. Everyone wants to win. It is *the will to pay the price* to win that makes winners.

REMEMBER: Today you need to continue to pay the price to win. Today, you have a full-time job—trying to find a job. Your hard labor at your job will pay off. God keeps His word; He will reward the work you do in faithfulness to Him.

PRAY: *Loving Father, make me diligent today. I want to be a winner. I want to do everything possible to ensure success in my job search. Enable me to "pay the price" so I may attain the desire of my heart—the job You have for me.*

PLAN: Write the words Pay the Price on a 3 x 5 card. Put it on your bathroom mirror as a reminder of Scripture's call to diligence.

14

LABOR FOR THE PROFIT

> All hard work brings a profit, but mere talk leads only to poverty.
>
> *Proverbs 14:23*

This has been a tough week. All your pavement-pounding and praying and hoping have resulted in no new leads. The temptation to lose hope and to doubt yourself, your worth, even God Himself, becomes greater when all your labor seems to produce nothing.

REMEMBER: The Word of God is not misleading. I must continue to do more than just talk about finding my next job. I must labor to find it if I am to labor in it.

PRAY: *Lord, give me the ability to keep "pounding the pavement" even when it is the last thing I want to do.*

Help me to continue until I find the job that will glorify You and meet my financial obligations.

PLAN: I will memorize this verse. And I will spend at least eight hours today looking for the job God has prepared for me.

15

PAVE THE WAY TO THE NEXT JOB

A gentle answer turns away wrath, but a harsh word stirs up anger.

Proverbs 15:1

Perhaps half of the divorces in America could have been prevented if a couple had applied this verse throughout their marriage. A gentle and kind word when every emotion of your heart cries out for an angry venting of your frustration may not be easy, but it is the right thing to do. And it just may pave the way to your next job.

REMEMBER: Most employers, believe it or not, appreciate grace under fire. A harsh word, even about a previous employer, may stir up anger toward you. Remember to keep your speech above reproach.

PRAY: *Lord of the gracious Word, strengthen me in the task of giving a gentle word when my emotions cry out with anything but gentleness.*

PLAN: Be kind with the words you use today.

16

FIND THE RIGHT PLAN

When a man's ways are pleasing to the LORD, he makes even his enemies live at peace with him. In his heart a man plans his course, but the Lord determines his steps.

Proverbs 16:7, 9

Make your plan and work your plan—but be prepared, for God sometimes makes other plans. Napoleon had to learn that lesson. He once flippantly said, "God was on the side of the army with the heaviest artillery." Later in life, exiled on the island of St. Helena, he had a more sobering assessment: "Man proposes; but God disposes."

REMEMBER: Set your heart on pleasing the Lord of your life. His plan is always better than yours—even though sometimes you may have doubts.

PRAY: *Sovereign Lord, sometimes I fear Your plan. I know I shouldn't, but I do. Today I'm afraid because I can't figure out what You are trying to teach me. And I'm afraid when I do find out, I'm not going to like it. Help me to trust You. Help me to let You direct my steps today.*

PLAN: Today, when my plan gets thrown off schedule, I will thank God for the detour even if I don't understand the reason.

17

Find a Biblical Friend

A friend loves at all times, and a brother is born for adversity.

Proverbs 17:17

Tough times and tough people don't always travel together. Often the tough times come when we are weakest. That's when a biblically-defined friend is needed.

A biblical friend is a friend who knows the tune of your life and is able to sing it when you have forgotten the melody. A biblical friend is born, created by a loving God, for times like an unexpected job loss and a difficult job search.

REMEMBER: God placed this verse in the Bible for a reason. He wanted you to know that you need a friend in the hard times of life. God knows your need better than you do.

PRAY: *Father and Friend, I need some friends who will help keep my vision of You and my job search clear. Help me to share my need with the friends I have. Give them wisdom in directing my vision. Raise up a special friend to help me through this time.*

PLAN: I am going to speak with one of my best friends and ask them to pray for me on a daily basis until I find a job.

18

Keep Your Head and Your Heart

A man's spirit sustains him in sickness, but a crushed spirit who can bear?

Proverbs 18:14

Your first feelings after losing your job were anger. Then your anger was joined by feelings of betrayal. That anger and betrayal dwell in your life, and now a new feeling has arisen—fear. You wonder, *Will I ever get another job?* The combination of all those feelings threatens to overwhelm you at times. Yet you know that if you are going to get another job you have got to deal with your anger, your sense of betrayal, and your fear.

REMEMBER: Keep your spirit, your heart, centered in the character of God. A heart centered in the character of God will be sustained through the trauma of a job loss and the search for a new job.

PRAY: *Father, renew my spirit today. Keep it from being crushed by my circumstances. Make the whole of my life declare that it will not be conquered. Let each interviewer see a resilience in me that causes them to give a second look at my resumé.*

PLAN: Have you scheduled time off just to relax since you lost your job? Plan at least two days off in the next two weeks.

19

Maintain Your Integrity II

Better a poor man whose walk is blameless than
a fool whose lips are perverse.

Proverbs 19:1

"If I have been injured by another, let me think [to] myself—How much better to be the sufferer than the wrongdoer!" Robert Cleaver Chapman (1803–1903) spoke these wise words on the importance of being forgiving and being a blessing to those who spitefully use us. He could easily have been commenting on the verse above or perhaps 1 Peter 3:9, "Do not repay evil with evil or insult with insult, but with blessing."

REMEMBER: No employer will hire a person who is unable to find anything good to say about his previous job or supervisor. It is important to keep your speech free of the bitterness that repels. Make it your aim to walk a blameless path in what you say.

PRAY: *Father, keep me from rutting my own path with words spoken harshly or out of turn. Help me to walk in forgiveness, kindness, and integrity rather than resentment.*

PLAN: In each interview today, use only positive terms in any references to your previous job, and end each interview with a polite and sincere thank-you from the heart.

20

The Sluggard Returns!

A sluggard does not plow in season; so at harvest time he looks but finds nothing.

Proverbs 20:4

The stranger happens upon a farmer and the two exchange howdy's. Says the stranger to the farmer, "How's things?"

"Tolerable," comes the reply. "Two weeks ago a tornado knocked down all the trees I had to chop down for this winter's firewood. Last week lightning struck the brush I was goin' to have to burn to clear the fields for planting."

The impressed stranger replies, "That's incredible. What are you doing now?"

The farmer answers, "Waiting for an earthquake to come along and shake the 'taters out of the ground."

Life doesn't work that way.

REMEMBER: You have to keep plowing the field if you are going to have a harvest. Hang in there. Your work will produce a crop. The job offer you want is coming. You just have to keep irrigating the field with your prayers and your honest efforts. God will reward.

PRAY: *Father of the harvest, I have plowed the want ads, pounded the pavement, and pursued every lead You have shown me—and I have found nothing. But I trust in You that the harvest season has just not yet arrived. Bring the harvest in soon, Lord. My family needs me to be gainfully employed.*

PLAN: Read Proverbs 6:7–11. Take time to laugh for a moment, but then focus your mind on the goals you need to accomplish today.

21

TRUST A POWERFUL GOD

The king's heart is in the hand of the Lord; he directs it like a watercourse wherever he pleases.

Proverbs 21:1

You've followed up on every lead given to you by friends. You've perused the want ads for weeks. You've read the Yellow Pages looking for new places to apply for jobs in your area. You've worn out your shoes, your spouse's patience, and your own left ear with a zillion phone calls and job interviews. Still, nothing. It is getting harder and harder to keep your motivation and hope at a productive level.

REMEMBER: God has not had a power outage. He is still the sovereign God of the universe. He is still able to work on your behalf. Trust Him to exercise His power at the perfect time.

PRAY: *Father, with every day that goes by, I am tempted to lose hope. Lift my spirit today. By Your great power, enable me to continue to do what must be done to find the job You have for me.*

PLAN: Today I will trust that God is still on my side and that He is already working to accomplish more than I am able to see.

22

Avoid Debt

> The rich rule over the poor, and the borrower is servant to the lender.
>
> *Proverbs 22:7*

With a clarity you never imagined, this Scripture speaks loudly to you at this juncture in your life. Since the loss of your job, the house payment, the credit card balance, and the electric company have become daily reminders that debt makes us slaves to the ones we owe.

REMEMBER: During this lean time it is important that you not take on new debt. Cut your expenses. Greater debt will pour cold water on your hope.

PRAY: *Gracious Father, give me creativity in navigating through this time. Help me to live a disciplined life and to not take on more debt than is necessary.*

PLAN: Set up an appointment with a pastor or elder of your church and ask for advice in restructuring your debt.

23

Avoid Bad Company

Do not join those who drink too much wine or gorge themselves on meat, for drunkards and gluttons become poor, and drowsiness clothes them in rags.

Proverbs 23:20–21

The apostle Paul might have been paraphrasing this verse when he wrote, "Do not be misled: 'Bad company corrupts good character'" (1 Cor. 15:33). A lifestyle centered around alcohol will eventually lead to poverty. Funny how the beer commercials never tell you that.

REMEMBER: Make sure you pursue relationships with the people of God. None of them are perfect, but you need the fellowship of people who are making progress in the grace and knowledge of God. Your health, your thinking, your budget, and your future will be much better off.

PRAY: *Father, surround me with Your people. Help me to be wise in the selection of my friends and the discipline of my habits.*

PLAN: Determine to neither eat nor drink to excess. Make this determination a commitment to your spouse or a good friend and ask them to hold you accountable.

24

OUT OF BED AND INTO THE SHOWER!

I went past the field of the sluggard, past the vineyard of the man who lacks judgment; thorns had come up everywhere, the ground was covered with weeds, and the stone wall was in ruins.

I applied my heart to what I observed and learned a lesson from what I saw.

Proverbs 24:30–32

REMEMBER: The image of the sluggard is the biblical equivalent of the modern-day couch potato. And the biblical antidote for couch-potatoitis is this: "I applied my heart to what I observed and I learned a lesson from what I saw." Benjamin Franklin addressed this idea by saying, "Well done is better than well said."

PRAY: *Father, sometimes I just don't feel like getting started. The effort seems so pointless in light of recent disappointments. Strengthen my resolve today so that I can avoid the destiny of the sluggard. Help me to apply what I am learning.*

PLAN: From this day forward, I am going to set my alarm in light of what I need to accomplish the next day. When the alarm goes off, my feet are going to hit the floor.

25

Over-Promotion Pitfalls I

Like clouds and wind without rain is a man who boasts of gifts he does not give.

Proverbs 25:14

The clouds and wind promise rain to the farmer's moisture-starved fields. When the former is not followed by the latter, the farmer is bitterly disappointed. Your employer will be disappointed as well if you proclaim in your interview more than you are capable of delivering.

REMEMBER: Your need for a job is not worth the price of your integrity or the humiliation you will feel when the boss finds out you can't do what he hired you to do. In the marketing arena there is a saying: Nothing kills a *good* product faster than *great* advertising. Be honest about your skills. God will honor your decision.

PRAY: *Lord, help me to answer wisely and honestly today about my knowledge and skills. Help my interviewer to see that I am the right person for the job, even if there are some skills or experience that I might still need to gain.*

PLAN: I am going to talk honestly about my strengths today. I am not going to boast about things that I cannot deliver.

26

Over-Promotion Pitfalls II

Do you see a man wise in his own eyes? There is more hope for a fool than for him.

Proverbs 26:12

A noted educator once said that when a life is wrapped up in itself it makes a very small package. Excessive pride, over-promotion, and conceit are diseases of the spirit—very unique diseases. They are the only diseases known to man that make everyone sick—except the one who has them.

REMEMBER: Honest humility, not false humility, is a trait that always attracts others, while pride almost always repels. Whatever your knowledge level, there will always be more that you could learn. The greater the island of knowledge, the greater the shores of ignorance as well.

PRAY: *Wise and gracious Lord, enable me to grow in honest humility today. Keep me from minimizing my strengths, but keep me from over-promoting them as well.*

PLAN: I will ask a good friend to do a mock interview with me today. I will then ask for an objective evaluation of my presentation that will enable me to avoid both overstatement and understatement of my knowledge and abilities.

27

Work Your Network

Let another praise you, and not your own mouth; someone else, and not your own lips.

Proverbs 27:2

You've thought it, haven't you? *If he is so good, why do I only hear about it from him?* A second thought often follows: *If he were as good as he says, others would be telling his story.* Anyone who needs to trumpet his or her own horn is probably more blow than show.

REMEMBER: The people who love and respect you are your best salesforce. Let *them* tell your story.

PRAY: *Father, use my friends in the process of this search. If they have friends who work in my skill and experience areas, help them to remember my need and mention my name.*

PLAN: Reread devotion 10, "Know When to Be Silent."

28

Be Patient

A faithful man will be richly blessed, but one eager to get rich will not go unpunished.

Proverbs 28:20

Are these your thoughts? *I'm not getting enough interviews. What am I doing wrong? Why am I not getting more second interviews? Is there something wrong with me? Is there something God is trying to teach me that I am not learning?*

REMEMBER: Everyone searching for a job has similar thoughts. Yes, you can hone your interviewing skills. Yes, God may be trying to teach you something. But remember, the Lord blesses diligence. Be patient. He will withhold no good thing from those who walk uprightly (see Ps. 84:11).

PRAY: *Ever-faithful Lord, make me diligent. Make me patient and faithful in the pursuit of my next job.*

PLAN: Today, thank God for how long it is taking you to find a new job.

29

CONTROL YOUR EMOTIONS

> A fool gives full vent to his anger, but a wise man keeps himself under control.
>
> *Proverbs 29:11*

Your spouse never knew what triggered it. Maybe it was just a question, perhaps even unspoken: "How did your job hunt go today?" Your explosion of anger opened the door to a chilling air that has brought with it an additional vapor of guilt and humiliation.

REMEMBER: A wise man is a man in control of his emotions. There are enough fools in the world without adding yourself to the rolls. Keep your anger and resentment in check. Take your cares to the One who understands them completely and ask Him for the power to hold your tongue.

PRAY: *Lord, make me a Spirit-directed and controlled believer. Help me to turn to You and then to turn aside when the temptation rises to vent my anger.*

PLAN: Read Ephesians 5:15–21. Make a point to confess and ask forgiveness from whomever you may have injured in your last loss of temper.

30

BUILD A BETTER FUTURE

Every word of God is flawless; he is a shield to those who take refuge in him.

Proverbs 30:5

Why doesn't God help me out?
He doesn't care…
God wants me to go through something awful…
God doesn't hear my prayers…
Maybe prayer doesn't work…
I've been a fool to trust God to provide for my needs…

Sometimes we have stupid thoughts.

REMEMBER: Every word of God is flawless (see 2 Tim. 3:16–17). A better future is built on the sure and steady foundation of Him and His Word. There is a promising future in following God's Word.

PRAY: *Father, I have neglected Your Word for so much of my life. Thank You for using my search for a job to deepen my dependence upon You and Your Word. Sustain my study of Your Word after the journey of the search ends.*

PLAN: Go to a Christian bookstore and purchase a simple study guide for one book of the Bible.

31

There Are Others Like You

Speak up for those who cannot speak for themselves, for the rights of all who are destitute. Speak up and judge fairly; defend the rights of the poor and needy.

Proverbs 31:8–9

Your search may not be over, but it is not too early to think about the new things you are learning in the process. You have gained skills and perspective in your experience of losing and searching for a job that others need.

REMEMBER: A believer in Christ never belongs to himself. All of his or her gifts, talents, abilities, and experiences are to be brought into the service of the King and His subjects. You have responsibilities to the body of Christ because of the experience you have gained in your search for a job.

PRAY: *Father, I still have so much to learn myself, but if You want to use me to help others, I'm ready to be used.*

PLAN: This Sunday I will ask my pastor if someone else who is looking for a job might need encouragement.

EPILOGUE

SURVIVING THE CHAOS OF THE HUNT

Betty and Carol and Bob have all found jobs.

For Betty, the process included a temporary job where she was under-challenged both in skills and intellect. She was viewed with jealousy by some and disdain by others. But the weeks of hunting, praying, calling, and trusting paid off. She landed a job in her area of specialty and is now digging her way out of the financial pit caused by her unemployment.

For Carol, the initial shock of rejection was tempered days later when her supervisor called to say that he was willing to work around her schedule. She breathed a sigh of relief, went back to work, but wondered when the axe would fall again.

Bob also found another job—with another food processing plant. The new job necessitated the sale of his home, a move to another state, and a cut in pay. But the work is challenging and the opportunities for advancement are promising.

Before he left for his new job, God used Bob in the life of Kyle, a research scientist also cut in the downsizing of federal programs. Kyle had been pounding the pavement from Chicago to Phoenix to Paris, France, for more than four months. To cut expenses his wife and children moved in with his mother in Arizona while Kyle wrapped up things in Chicago and tried to feed his family.

Loneliness, defeat, rejection, and joylessness had become his constant companions—until Bob offered understanding and the rough draft of this book to bring new perspective and hope back into Kyle's life.

Kyle and Carol and Bob and Betty have learned to survive through the chaos of the hunt. As a result, each has grown and found gainful employment.

Management consultant and best-selling author Tom Peters writes perceptively about coping with the ever-changing challenges of business at the approach of the 21st century:

> To thrive "amidst" chaos means to cope or come to grips with it, to succeed in spite of it. But that is too reactive an approach, and misses the point. The true objectivity is to take the chaos as given and learn to thrive *on* it. The winners of tomorrow will deal *proactively* with chaos, will look at the chaos per se as the source of market advantage, not as a problem to be got around.

These principles apply just as easily to finding a job. Being successful in the hunt for a new job takes more than "dealing with" or "coping with" or "tolerating" the chaos of being without a job. To win at this game you have to learn to "thrive on" it. You have to learn to make it work for you. The apostle James' approach is relevant here.

> Consider it all joy, my brethren, when you encounter various trials, knowing that the testing of your faith produces endurance. And let endurance have *its* perfect result, that you may be perfect and complete, lacking in nothing.
>
> *James 1:2–4, NASB*

The Living Bible paraphrase captures the spirit of the verse well. When you encounter various trials, "welcome them as friends," it says. Admittedly, putting out the welcome mat for a job loss is not an easy task, but the promise of Scripture is that such a way of life will be rewarded.

As a job seeker, you will have days that are absurdly chaotic. You've been out of a job for two months so you have little money to work with. As a result you hesitate to put too much money where you can't get to it quickly—like into your gas tank or for a new muffler. But today you have a job interview and have to stop and buy gas. One delay. As you leave the station, the police pull you over for noise from that broken muffler. A second delay. Now you are running

Epilogue: Surviving the Chaos of the Hunt / 41

late for the interview, so you exceed the speed limit and fear being stopped for speeding. You don't get caught, but you *do* arrive at the interview ten minutes late with a bead of sweat dripping down the small of your back. You don't take even a moment to pray and compose yourself so as to make the best possible presentation of yourself and your skills. There will be days like that in life—with or without a job.

Place your hope in Christ. You will never be disappointed with Him. King David, the sweet psalmist of Israel, starts the song that believers in God have echoed for three thousand years:

> I will instruct you and teach you in the way which you should go; I will counsel you with My eye upon you.
>
> *Psalm 32:8,* NASB

God knows your situation. He will counsel you from His Word and through His people "with His eye upon you"—that is, with an intimate knowledge of who you are and what you need. It always pays to place your trust in Him. Know that "The joy of the Lord is your strength" (Neh. 8:10) during this trying time in your life. King Solomon had some advice for how to organize a life to survive the quandaries and surprises.

> Divide your portion to seven, or even to eight, for you do not know what misfortune may occur on the earth. If the clouds are full, they pour

out rain upon the earth; and whether a tree falls toward the south or toward the north, wherever it falls, there it lies. He who watches the wind will not sow and he who looks at the clouds will not reap.

Just as you do not know the path of the wind and how bones are formed in the womb of the pregnant woman, so you do not know the activity of God who makes all things.

Ecclesiastes 11:2–5, NASB

Solomon seems to be saying that we each have to deal with life the way it comes at us. First prepare for the possibility of misfortune. Second, don't whine about the "if only's." And third, don't put all your eggs in one basket.

My hope and prayer is that these devotions will help you find Him in the center of your trial, and that in finding Him, you will find hope for the journey.

RESOURCES

Suggested Reading

Bolles, Richard Nelson. *1994 What Color Is Your Parachute?* Berkley, Calif.: Ten Speed Press, 1994.

Briles, Judith, Luci Swindoll, and Mary Welchel. *Workplace Questions Women Ask.* Multnomah, Ore.: Multnomah Press.

Elandson, Douglas. *Job Shuffle.* Chicago, Ill.: Moody Press.

Bramlett, James. *Finding Work* (audio tape). Grand Rapids, Mich.: Zondervan Publishing House, 1988.

Ellis, Lee. *Job Search Strategies.* Chicago, Ill.: Moody Press, 1993.

Hosier, Helen. *Suddenly Unemployed: How to Survive Unemployment and Land a Better Job!* San Bernardino, Calif.: Here's Life Publishers, 1992.

Larson, Dale and Sandy. *Patching Your Parachute: How You Can Beat Unemployment.* Downers Grove, Ill.: InterVarsity Press.

Lensmith, Lawrence. *Persuasive Resume!* Oconomowoc, Wis.: Desktop Impressions, Inc., 1991, 1993.

MacMillan, Pat. *Hiring Excellence.* Colorado Springs, Colo.: NavPress.

Morton, Tom. *The Survivor's Guide to Unemployment*. Colorado Springs, Colo.: Pinon Press, 1992.

Partow, Donna. *Homemade Business: A Woman's Step-by-Step Guide to Earning Money at Home.* Colorado Springs, Colo.: Focus on the Family Press.

Siedle, Robert D. *Quick Job Hunt Guide: Unique Ways to Land that Job.* Lancaster, Pa.: Starburst, 1991.

Smith, Fred. *You and Your Network.* Waco, Tex.: Word Books, 1984.